ideals

AUTUMN TIME ISSUE

The pleasant sun-filled days of summer pass
And usher in the dazzling autumn time,
A time of harvest when the earth is prime,
A time of beauty nothing can surpass.

The hills and valleys are a showy mass
Of vivid colors startling and sublime;
They blend, then clash, in nature's pantomime:
The reds and yellows, violet and brass.

This is a test of earth's transcendent schemes:
Were plowing, planting, tending all for naught?
Were springtime hopes and plans but empty dreams
Which in our summer labor we forgot?

No, Autumn in her majesty redeems
And makes the earth a special, sacred spot.

Ruth G. Rothe

Managing Editor, Ralph Luedtke
Associate Editor, Julie Hogan
Photographic Editor, Gerald Koser
Production Editor, Stuart L. Zyduck

ISBN 0-89542-310-3 250

IDEALS—Vol. 34, No. 5—September, MCMLXXVII. Published bimonthly by IDEALS PUBLISHING CORP., 11315 Watertown Plank Road, Milwaukee, Wis. 53226. Second-class postage paid at Milwaukee, Wisconsin. Copyright © MCMLXXVII by IDEALS PUBLISHING CORP. All rights reserved. Title IDEALS registered U.S. Patent Office.

ONE YEAR SUBSCRIPTION—six consecutive issues as published—only $10.00
TWO YEAR SUBSCRIPTION—twelve consecutive issues as published—only $17.00
SINGLE ISSUES—only $2.50

Fall Arrived

Yes, Fall arrived this morning.
　I felt her tangy touch
Persuading me to wander
　Down paths I love so much.

The lovely trees were spilling
　Gold parchments at my feet,
And each one represented
　A memory so sweet.

I thought of friends and loved ones;
　With recollecting smile,
To days of tender childhood,
　My mind went back awhile.

I paused amid earth's beauty
　To lift my heart in praise,
To thank God for the blessing
　Of these autumnal days.

Yes, Fall arrived this morning.
　I felt her tangy touch
Persuading me to wander
　Down paths I love so much.

Georgia B. Adams

Sheep Feeding Time at Thoms' Farm
EATON CENTER, NEW HAMPSHIRE
Cyr Color Photo Agency

I followed October's trail today.
It led through the woods and far away
To the purple hills where a vapor rose
Which only a day in October knows.

The leaves, all poised for instant flight,
Seemed to hold their breath while awaiting night;
And all were garbed in their fancy best
For one last fling ere their winter's rest.

The squirrels were garnering nuts away,
Oh! what a bounteous harvest day!
And over the treetops I saw them fly—
The wild geese honking a last good-bye.

The stately maples with leaves now thin
All testified where October had been,
And the crispy crunch as I walked along
Was the thrilling theme of October's song.

Mary E. Linton

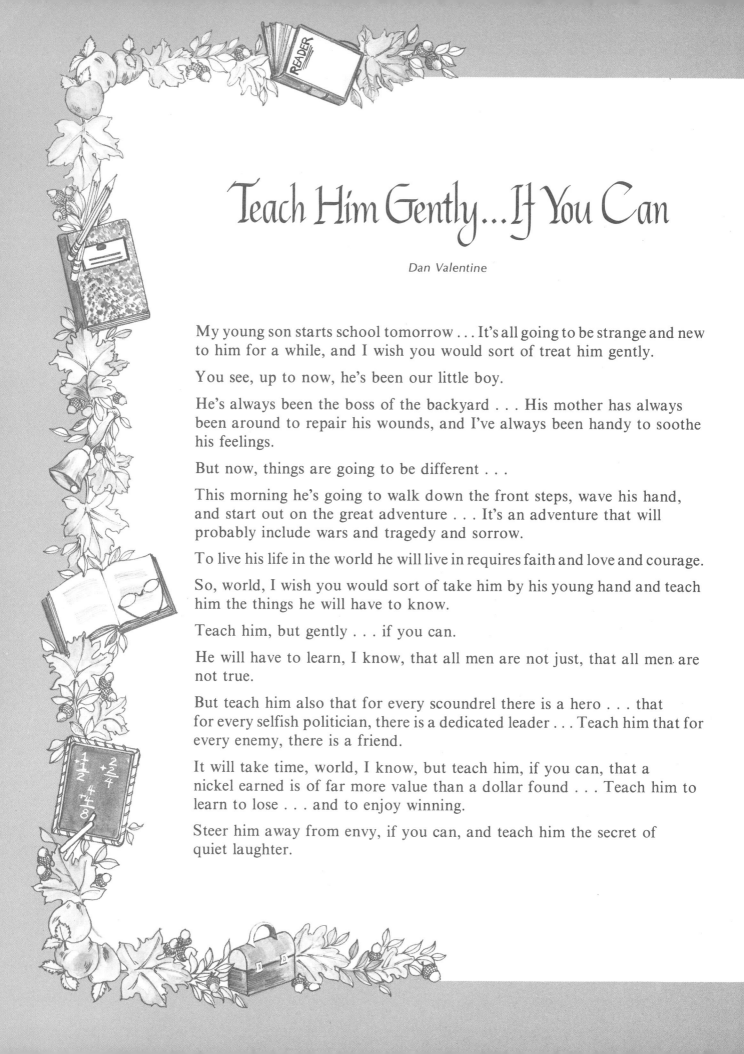

Teach Him Gently...If You Can

Dan Valentine

My young son starts school tomorrow . . . It's all going to be strange and new to him for a while, and I wish you would sort of treat him gently.

You see, up to now, he's been our little boy.

He's always been the boss of the backyard . . . His mother has always been around to repair his wounds, and I've always been handy to soothe his feelings.

But now, things are going to be different . . .

This morning he's going to walk down the front steps, wave his hand, and start out on the great adventure . . . It's an adventure that will probably include wars and tragedy and sorrow.

To live his life in the world he will live in requires faith and love and courage.

So, world, I wish you would sort of take him by his young hand and teach him the things he will have to know.

Teach him, but gently . . . if you can.

He will have to learn, I know, that all men are not just, that all men are not true.

But teach him also that for every scoundrel there is a hero . . . that for every selfish politician, there is a dedicated leader . . . Teach him that for every enemy, there is a friend.

It will take time, world, I know, but teach him, if you can, that a nickel earned is of far more value than a dollar found . . . Teach him to learn to lose . . . and to enjoy winning.

Steer him away from envy, if you can, and teach him the secret of quiet laughter.

Let him learn early that the bullies are the easiest people to lick . . . Teach him, if you can, the wonder of books . . . But also give him quiet time to ponder the eternal mystery of birds in the sky, bees in the sun and flowers on a green hillside.

In school, world, teach him it is far more honorable to fail than to cheat . . . Teach him to have faith in his own ideas, even if everyone tells him they are wrong . . . Teach him to be gentle with gentle people and tough with tough people.

Try to give my son the strength not to follow the crowd when everyone else is getting on the bandwagon . . . Teach him to listen to all men . . . But teach him also to filter all the hearts on a screen of truth and take only the good that comes through.

Teach him, if you can, how to laugh when he is sad . . . Teach him there is no shame in tears . . . Teach him there can be glory in failure and despair in success.

Teach him to scoff at cynics and to beware of too much sweetness . . . Teach him to sell his brawn and brains to the highest bidders but never to put a tag on his heart and soul.

Teach him to close his ears to a howling mob . . . and to stand and fight if he thinks he's right.

Treat him gently, world, but don't coddle him, because only the test of fire makes fine steel.

Let him have the courage to be impatient . . . let him have the patience to be brave.

Teach him always to have sublime faith in himself. Because then he will always have sublime faith in mankind.

This is a big order, world, but see what you can do . . . He's such a fine little fellow, my son!

Indian Summer

Indian summer in the forest
  Is enchantment to behold
When the birch leaves turn to yellow
  And the maple's red and gold.

The dark green of the hemlock
  And the fragrance of the pines
And errant rays of sunshine
  In long and slanting lines.

Still there is more enchantment
  In this scene with charm replete,
'Tis the whirr of feathery pinions
  And the patter of scurrying feet.

It is the little folk of the forest
  That love to romp and play,
Or store up their cache of treasure
  For a cold and wintry day,

The sudden flight of the partridge,
  The squirrels with their bushy tails,
The ever cautious rabbits
  Mapping their winter trails.

We are thankful for such beautiful scenes,
  Our hearts fill with delight,
And pleasant memories linger
  While the scene turns sparkling white.

Wenzel A. Seiler

Photo opposite
CONEJOS CANYON, COLORADO
Taurus Photos

When the frost was on the pumpkin,
And the birds had flown away,
Then 'twas time again for husking
And you'd hear my father say;

"I must get that corn in, Mother,
So as we can have a bee."
And she'd answer, "Yes, sir, Father,
Any night's all right with me."

Shocks of corn soon filled the barn floor,
There were lanterns hanging high,
As we hurried with the milking;
Folks would soon be dropping by.

Then the sturdy rafters echoed
With their laughter and their song,
And the hours of work went quickly,
They were never very long.

I remember, I remember,
Oh, how well I see it all,
I was then a lad of twenty
Brown of face, but straight and tall.

I was husking with the others
Then I shouted, "Look, red ear!"
And I held it high, then higher,
Though my knees felt kind of queer.

Every face turned toward Miss Sally;
Oh, just see her smile and blush.
She's the fairest at the party,
You could almost hear folks hush.

I went forth and claimed *two* kisses,
What a happy pair we made;
As right there at that husking
Springtime wedding plans were made.

Phyllis C. Michael

FIND THE RED EAR

R. J. McGinnis

A shrewd Yankee farmer thought up the husking bee to get his corn husked free. His was a simple idea, but the fascinating by-products soon got out of hand and the husking bee became a social institution which spread to all parts of the country where corn was grown.

It was the custom in old New England to haul the corn out of the field before the winter set in and store it in the barn. The farmer husked it at his leisure, protected from the elements.

Husking bees were usually held in the late fall before the weather got too cold for comfort in an unheated barn. Neighbors gathered, sat on stools, and husked the corn, throwing the ears in the center of the floor. Near the door was a table laden with plates of doughnuts and cookies, and jugs of cider. Constant reference was made to these refreshments by the huskers.

A gentleman finding a red ear of corn was privileged to kiss the lady of his choice. This custom was sometimes abused by unscrupulous swains who smuggled red ears to a husking under their coats and brought them out at the strategic moment. Many a troth was plighted at a husking bee.

At the better husking bees the evening was rounded off by a square dance. This was the ancestor of the effete barn dance of modern times, a pale substitute for the real thing, which not only provided a good time, but got the corn husked as well.

Phil Slaske

Highbush
Cranberry

Lynn Stone

Blue Gentian

Lynn Stone

Bittersweet

Autumn Farewell

Blue gentians in the woodlot,
Blue haze along the hill,
Gray smoke among the timber,
A lonely warbler's trill—
Red sumac on the fence posts,
Late blooms (with heads held high)
Caress each fickle monarch
Waving autumn's last goodbye!

Edith Eckblad

Gathering Bittersweet

Bittersweet vines hang heavy
With their orange-red berries,
Part of the autumn's harvest
Like summer's red, ripe cherries.

The crooked country fences
Are laden with October's vines,
And the berry of the bittersweet
Hangs deep orange where it twines.

When the sun of noon grows warm,
And autumn clouds hang still,
We go to pick the bittersweet
Across the meadow, over the hill.

Lucille Crumley

The mums that march beside the path
   Are much like little girls;
Some come with hair cut short and neat
   While others come in curls.

Chrysanthemums

No matter how they choose to come,
   They bring a charming grace
With color bright and warmth to add
   To Autumn's smiling face.

Like little girls on sturdy legs,
   They preen there in the sun.
No wonder that they proudly smile;
   They're lovely, every one.

Each little mum beside the path,
   Lift up your beaming face
Till snowflakes fall to wrap you round
   Like softly swirling lace.

Josephine Millard

The Frontier of James Fenimore Cooper

The year 1789 was a year of firsts for the United States. The first President, George Washington, was inaugurated for his first term. He presided over a country with a new constitution, ratified only that year. And, finally, America's first major literary figure was born.

James Fenimore Cooper was born in Burlington, New Jersey, but soon moved to Ostego Lake in upstate New York where his father had bought a large tract of wilderness land. The lake and its environs provide the setting for many of his later writings.

Cooper entered Yale at the age of thirteen, but dropped out at the age of sixteen in order to go to sea. At nineteen, he was commissioned a midshipman in the Navy, but left that after three years to get married and settle down in New York.

Cooper would probably never have been other than a country gentleman if it had not been for a dare from his wife. When he exclaimed, upon reading an English novel, that he thought he could write a better one himself, his wife challenged him to try. His first attempt was a failure, but later tries produced great stories of adventure at sea (drawn from experiences when Cooper was a sailor) and the popular Leatherstocking Tales—stories of Indians and pioneers which chronicle the early days of the country and life on the frontier.

Cooper has been credited with giving the young country a legendary past of its own. His works have been translated into almost every language and were as popular in Europe as in America. All over the world, people came to know Cooper's hero, as a symbol of the independent, ingenious American. In the following excerpt from *The Deerslayer*, the hero, along with two women he is protecting, go to meet his Mohican friend and barely escape capture by hostile Mingos.

"Is the rock empty, Judith?" inquired Deerslayer, as soon as he had checked the drift of the ark, deeming it imprudent to venture unnecessarily near the shore. "Is anything to be seen of the Delaware chief?"

"Nothing, Deerslayer. Neither rock, shore, tree, nor lake seems to have ever held a human form."

"Keep close, Judith—keep close, Hetty—a rifle has a prying eye, a nimble foot, and a desperate fatal tongue. Keep close, then, but keep up actyve looks, and be on the alart. 'T would grieve me to the very heart did any harm befall either of you."

"And *you*, Deerslayer!" exclaimed Judith, turning her handsome face from the loop, to bestow a gracious and grateful look on the young man; "do *you* 'keep close,' and have a proper care that the savages do not catch a glimpse of you! A bullet might be as fatal to *you* as to one of us; and the blow that you felt would be felt by all."

"No fear of me, Judith—no fear of me, my good gal. Do not look this a way, although you look so pleasant and comely, but keep your eyes on the rock, and the shore, and the—"

Deerslayer was interrupted by a slight exclamation from the girl, who, in obedience, to his hurried gestures, as much as in obedience to his words, had immediately bent her looks again in the opposite direction.

"What is 't?—what is 't, Judith?" he hastily demanded. "Is anything to be seen?"

"There is a man on the rock!—an Indian warrior in his paint, and armed!"

"Where does he wear his hawk's feather?" eagerly added Deerslayer, relaxing his hold of the line, in readiness to drift nearer the place of rendezvous. "Is it fast to the war-lock, or does he carry it above the left ear?"

" 'T is as you say, above the left ear; he smiles and mutters the word 'Mohican.' "

"God be praised, 't is the Sarpent at last!" exclaimed the young man, suffering the line to slip through his hands, until hearing a light bound, in the other end of the craft, he instantly checked the rope, and began to haul it in again, under the assurance that his object was effected.

At that moment the door of the cabin was opened hastily, and a warrior, darting through the little room, stood at Deerslayer's side, simply uttering the exclamation "Hugh!" At the next instant Judith and Hetty shrieked, and the air was filled with the yell of twenty savages, who came leaping through the branches down the bank, some actually falling headlong into the water in their haste.

"Pull, Deerslayer!" cried Judith, hastily barring the door, in order to prevent an inroad by the passage through which the Delaware had just entered; "pull for life and death—the lake is full of savages wading after us!"

The young men—for Chingachgook immediately came to his friend's assistance—needed no second bidding; but they applied themselves to their task in a way that showed how urgent they deemed the occasion. The great difficulty was in suddenly overcoming the *vis inertia* of so large a mass; for once in motion, it was easy to cause the scow to skim the water with all the necessary speed.

"Pull, Deerslayer, for Heaven's sake!" cried Judith again at the loop. "These wretches rush into the water like hounds following their prey! Ah!—the scow moves! and now the water deepens to the armpits of the foremost; still they rush forward, and will seize the ark!"

A slight scream, and then a joyous laugh followed from the girl; the first produced by a desperate effort of their pursuers, and the last by its failure; the scow, which had now got fairly in motion, gliding ahead into deep water with a velocity that set the designs of their enemies at naught. As the two men were prevented by the position of the cabin from seeing what passed astern, they were compelled to inquire of the girls into the state of the chase.

"What now, Judith?—what next? Do the Mingos still follow, or are we quit of 'em for the present?" demanded Deerslayer, when he felt the rope yielding, as if the scow was going fast ahead, and heard the scream and the laugh of the girl almost in the same breath.

"They have vanished!—one, the last, is just burying himself in the bushes of the bank—there, he has disappeared in the shadows of the trees! You have got your friend, and we are all safe!"

Trees have a way of talking to us—oh, not in so many words. But they tell us things just the same—if we listen and observe and are still. A forest can be both cathedral and classroom to the receptive, and a single tree can furnish enough food for thought for the lifetime of man.

Esther Baldwin York

I traveled a land of painted trees,
   colored by autumn's hand,
On a carpet of gold, of russet and
   brown which covered the forest
   land.
I gathered the leaves which fell at my
   feet and tossed them into the sun,
And watched them float in the gentle
   breeze, seemingly full of fun.
I stopped and gazed at the blue of the
   skies through pillars of golden
   hue,
And noted approaching ships of the
   air reflecting the gold in the blue.
It was peaceful and calm in this silent
   lane where the carol of autumn
   was played.
And my heart sang out with thanks
   to God for this land which His
   hand had made.

Everett Wentworth Hill

Gathering Nuts in Fall

When summer is over and turned into fall;
When wild geese are honking; when bluejays call;
When mornings are crisp it is time then, I know;
The nut trees are loaded and it's time to go.

Then I love to remember the old-fashioned scene,
When we'd get bags and baskets and hitch up the team
And head for the woods, where we always knew
The walnuts, the beechnuts and hickory nuts grew.

For beechnuts we'd spread old sheets on the ground,
Then shake the limbs where the best nuts were found,
Then laugh with glee as the nuts start to shower,
Getting more in a minute than you could pick in an hour.

Getting walnuts and hickories was harder to do;
But with old clubs, which we accurately threw,
They rained down in plenty with a plupity-plup,
And waiting hands greedily gathered them up.

I love to recall those dear days of old,
When we gathered nuts we thought good as gold;
For they added a treat to a long, winter night,
As we ate nuts and apples where hearth fires burned bright.

Ernest Jack Sharpe

Autumn Leaves

I love to watch the autumn leaves
As they slowly tumble down;
I love to hear their crackling
As my feet trod o'er the ground.

A lovely carpet neath my feet
Is now formed by autumn leaves,
With color scattered everywhere
In the choicest pattern weaves.

I love to rake them in a heap
And to watch the children play;
For soon the color will be gone,
Replaced by snow someday.

Ruth H. Underhill

Autumn Pleasure

The autumn leaves are falling down
Like snow on countryside and town;
And little children laugh and shout
In colored leaf-drifts all about,
As reds and golds and greens and browns
Invite the active little clowns
To run and tumble to excess
In Indian summer's loveliness!

George L. Ehrman

Photo opposite
RAKING LEAVES IN NEWBERRY, VERMONT
Fred M. Dole

Now, as preserving season ends,
The housewife busily ascends
From cellarway to kitchen stove
And back into her treasure trove
Where, richly shining, there below,
In ruby light and amber glow,
The jelly glasses deeply line
The cellar like a jewel mine.

The labels stand out, starkly white,
Against the gloom of cellar night—
A Milky Way of earthbound stars
To light the dim expanse of jars.
The housewife needs them not, herself,
Whose fingers studded every shelf.
This is her jewel box, and she
Knows every gem by memory.

COUNTRY CELLAR

Mary Louise Cheatham

Between the briefly opened doors,
The exiled sun, in shafts, explores
And strikes a darkly purple vein;
Against the wall, a cherry stain,
And over near the farther stairs
The gold-white globules of the pears,
And lingers there, in happy stealth,
Upon this unexpected wealth.

She proudly eyes her damson plums—
(A season's worth of juice-sharp thumbs!)
And sets her last preserve hoard in—
(A summer's worth of fruit-stained skin!)
She fondly lets her glances fall
In one last gaze upon them all,
And then, preparing to depart,
She leaves with beauty in her heart.

Deep in New England woods are old gnarled trees
With apples called the "Beauty of the Air,"
And in the Indian summer haze their hue
Burns darkly overhead, serene and fair.

I have not seen them, yet if I should go
Beneath those trees some autumn day alone,
I would find apples, bathed in crystal light,
My mind has pictured and for long has known.

A Wild Apple

An apple eaten in the autumn wind
Holds all the virtue of the sun and frost;
So I would taste at once the apple's tang
For fear the wild sweet flavor would be lost.

He was a poet who once gave to this fruit
Warm syllables that gleam with beauty's flame,
And though his name is lost, his shining thought
Lives down all autumns in one shining name.

Reid Crowell

Gathering Apples

With our baskets and a ladder,
  To the orchard we gaily go,
To pick the scarlet-cheeked fruit
  Along the gnarled apple row.

The sun hangs like a brass kettle
  And gentians blow at our feet;
A breeze sweeps down from the north
  That, too, is apple sweet.

There is much talk and laughter
  As the baskets slowly fill;
Then, we head for our homestead
  At the bottom of the hill.

The fruit will be stored in the cellar,
  In mountains of flaming red,
To mellow for our daily treats
  On the cold, winter days ahead.

Earle J. Grant

Photo opposite
A. Devaney

from the
editor's scrapbook

Across the fields October flings
Handfuls of scarlet leaves;
And nature adds a golden thread
To the tapestry she weaves.

Bettie Payne Welles

God painted all the autumn leaves
And put to sleep the flowers,
And told the birds to find a place
To spend their winter hours.

Charles Bowman

He enjoys much who is thankful for little; a
grateful mind is both a great and a happy
mind.

Pierre Charron

Gratitude is a becoming trait. It sweetens life,
cements the bonds of friendship, gives cheer
to fellowship, and makes benevolence a joy.

James Henry Potts

Each one must make a quiet place
Within his heart, where he can go
To find himself and, for a space,
Drink deeply where still waters flow.

Inga Gilson Caldwell

Earth sitteth still, and is at rest.

Zechariah 1:11

Let us give thanks to God upon Thanksgiving Day. Nature is beautiful and fellowmen are dear, and duty is close beside us, and God is over us and in us.

Phillips Brooks

Behold congenial autumn comes,
The sabbath of the year!

Logan

Contentment consists not in great wealth but in few wants.

Epictetus

Cultivate the thankful spirit . . . it will be to thee a perpetual feast. There is, or ought to be, with us no such things as small mercies. A really thankful heart will extract motive for gratitude from everything, making the most of even scanty blessings.

Author Unknown

The door of autumn,
Gold on the one side,
Silver on the other—
Let us pass through softly.

Irene Stanley

A face without a smile is like a lantern without a light.

Ernest Reeves

By all these lovely tokens,
September days are here,
With summer's best of weather
And autumn's best of cheer.

Helen Hunt Jackson

A Dream of Autumn

Each tree wore gypsy ribbons in her hair
And dressed as gaily as any autumn wood,
And scattered leaves of russet,
    gold and brown
To tread upon in silence understood
By every butterfly and bird and bee,
As golden haze envelopes all the land
Where milkweed parachutes go
    sailing slowly by,
And make a noiseless landing near at hand.

Oh, liquid golden atmosphere sublime
Of autumn days and flowers and gourds,
Of streams turned red with nature's wine
And colors everywhere outpoured,
Of birds whose thoughts have
    southward turned
Though not ready for their migrant flight,
They wheel and soar against the evening sun
And mount to heights that take them
    out of sight.

Murmuring zephyrs tattling to the leaves
That fall like bits of calico upon the lake
Where wild ducks when they are startled
Beat their wings and quack and shake
The water from their feathers
E're they rise to fly in V formation,
For the reedy marshes of the southland
Is their distant winter destination.

Apple trees bend low with red
    and golden fruit
That's picked and piled in baskets high,
Then stored away in darkened cellars
To be eaten, when they're mellow,
    on a winter's night.
Along the road the goldenrod still blooms
And bees are yellow with the dusty gold,
Wild grapes twine round the old oak trees
And on a frosty morn are juicy,
    sweet and cold.

And o'er the meadows for the cows I went
And stopped to warm my feet where Daisy lay;
Across the hills I heard the cowbells clinkin'
And found a path through berry briars made.
Then home again; the sun has warmed the world,
The cows walk slowly to the barn;
And I before the fire shall sit and dream,
As autumn quietly enfolds the farm.

Helen Monnette

Little Spunk of

Down by the creek, there's a path
  you can follow
That winds through Goblin Gulch,
  near Halloween Hollow.
Halloween Hollow is a well-known school
  for night-flying bats,
  witches, ghosts,
  and big black cats!

To live in the Hollow, one must be
  so scary and mean
He can frighten even grown-ups
  on Halloween!
All cats must be as black as
  the night,
With dispositions to stir
  screech owls to fright.
Little Spunk was as black as
  the bottom of the sea,
But gentle—as only
  a kitten can be.

One morning, Little Spunk was aroused
  by a pounding sound.
He yawned, stretched, then peeked
  around.
Look! Wiggle Witch is putting up
  a great big sign!
"Eight Tonight—Broom Riding Lesson,"
  said the first line.
"All Black Cats MUST Attend,"
  the second line clearly read.

Little Spunk shuddered and wished
  he'd stayed in bed!
He wailed (mostly to himself),
  "I'm too scared to fly!
I know I'll fall as we zoom
  through the sky!
But I'm a cat—that means
  I have to go.
But wait! The sign says
  BLACK cats—so—
What if I weren't black, but a lovely white?
Then I wouldn't have to go
  broom-riding tonight!"
"Hoppin' hoot owl," he shouted,
  then on his way,
To the creaky barn haunted
  by Skeleton Grey.

A can of white paint stood high
  on the barn's dusty shelf.
He poked it, hoping to spill it
  all over himself.
Down came the empty paint can
  and three old pails,
Barely brushing his whiskers, and spilling
  not paint, but nails!

Halloween Hollow

"Wow! This place is spooky!
  I'd best be on my way,
'Cause I've got to get white before
  the end of this day!"

Scampering across the field, he cornered
  a friendly mouse
Who had just nibbled open a flour sack
  in the witch's house.
"A great idea! Flour power will sprinkle
  my coat furry white."
So tiptoeing up to the witch's back door,
  he stayed well out of sight.
Quietly he darted through the kitchen,
  popped into the flour sack.
He rolled over on his tummy—
  then on his back
And caught a glimpse of a fan
  cooling a blueberry pie.

While taking just one bite, the fan blew
  all his white into the sky!
And before he could dive again
  into the flour sack,
He heard the witch's broom—
  landing out back.

The witch spied him and quickly
  gave chase,
Just as Little Spunk got tangled
  in a freshly washed pillowcase.
Wrapped in white, he tumbled
  down Pumpkin Slope,
Skidding to a stop at the washhouse,
  in a bucket of soap!

Seeing a broken mirror, he hobbled
  over that way.
He saw only himself and the pillowcase
  in complete disarray.
"Hard as I try, I'll never be
  a lovely white.
It's time to be brave and go broom
  riding tonight."

Little Spunk, tail held high, arrived
  proudly on time.
He bravely took his place at the end
  of the long, long line.
When his turn came to face the head witch
  of the school,
She gazed down her long nose at him, from
  a three-legged stool.
"Great ghost! You're no CAT, but a kitten!
  Flying doesn't make sense,
You should be keeping pumpkins company
  on the cornfield fence!"

So, if you're brave enough to sneak down
  by the creek this Halloween night,
Listen carefully—you may hear Little Spunk
  howling at the bats in the moonlight!

Arlene Cook

Many times we've reaped and gathered the glowing harvest yield . . . the burnished fruit and orange pumpkins . . . the yellow gold of ripened fields . . . We've thrilled to see the corn in tassel and the heavy apple boughs . . . and stood in grateful silence beneath a bulging mow.

Many times we've strolled where red and gold still lingered on the hill . . . where acorns crunched beneath our feet . . . and flaming trees stood silent, still . . . Many times we've found a quiet place to reap the blessings of the year . . . to gather in the warmth of smiles . . . the thoughtful words and moments dear . . . A quiet place where we could dream of fruitful deeds that mellowed long . . . of seeds of kindness that were sown . . . that blossomed into grateful song.

Many times we've lingered there alone, from all the world apart . . . to thank God for His love and care . . . and reap the treasures of the heart.

Joy Belle Burgess

John Slobodnik

It's Halloween Again

Halloween is here again
With golden pumpkins all about;
Goblins now will come a-spying,
Witches through the air a-flying,
Funny faces we'll be buying;
At dark of night we'll all go out.

Halloween is here again . . .
Autumn leaves come tumbling down,
Black cats will slink about tonight,
The moon will shed an eerie light;
"Trick or treat" will bring delight
From every house in town.

We all look forward to the time
When Halloween is here,
Owls will hoot high in the trees
And we will brave the chilly breeze
That heralds winter's coming freeze . . .
October's time of year.

So join me on this special night
When ghostlike shapes are seen;
We'll duck for apples, spin the pan,
Play blindman's buff and tag our man,
Pull taffy, fragrant, golden tan . . .
This night of Halloween.

Eleanor Elkins

There is one pleasure
I like to recall . . .
Bobbing for apples,
How that amused one and all!
We were bound and determined
Into the apples to bite,
As they kept floating around
To everyone's delight.

In a huge wooden bucket
The apples would bob
As we filled it with water
Clear up to the top;
And many a time
A dousing we'd get,
While some happy prankster
Would shout "Let's get wet!"
And push our eager faces
Deep down in the tub,
We'd come up gasping,
Not expecting that dub!

Bobbing for Apples

On through the years
This sport can be seen,
On the festive occasion
Of each Halloween.
A faint wisp of smile
Comes o'er my face,
As I muse for a moment
How I tried to embrace
A floating red apple
Between my set teeth,
But somehow or other
I never accomplished that feat.

Ann Schneider

Jack-O'-Lantern

We have a knife and pumpkin, so
We're ready to begin.
To carve Jack's jolly eyes and nose
And shape his friendly grin.

We feel extremely proud of him,
In just a little while,
Because he has such shining eyes
And such a beaming smile.

Gail Brook Burket

When a jack-o'-lantern sits in the window at night,
It tells a gay fable with its flickering light
Of tricking-and-treating and stories homespun
About witches and goblins and cats on the run.

It tells of the lads who down on the farms
Picked the best pumpkins and carried in arms,
So other little children could cut them so neat
And make a gay face for a Halloween treat.

Now goblins and games and parties are fine,
But give me a bright jack-o'-lantern for mine,
To put in my window on a cool autumn night
To tell about Halloween with its flickering light.

Laurie E. Dawson

Roadside Stand

I love to visit roadside stands
   When autumn fills the air—
A grand array of sights and scents
   Is waiting for me there.

There are rosy, red-cheeked apples
   In baskets all around,
And bright orange pumpkins, big and small,
   Lie heaped upon the ground.

The jugs of cider stand in rows
   Like liquid burnished gold;
The Indian corn hung all about
   Is lovely to behold.

There's nothing I can think of that
   Can truly quite compare
With roadside stands in autumn and
   Their harvest beauty, rare.

Peggy Mlcuch

Now that autumn has candy-glazed the land,
We go motoring and seek the roadside stand;
For it is always a pleasure to behold
Baskets of red apples and the pumpkins gold.

We buy jars of jam, jelly and marmalade
Amid chrysanthemums that are like rare brocade,
Orange-red bittersweet berries cluster there,
And spicy marigolds scent the autumn air.

There are bunches of Indian corn so gay
And sprays of Chinese lanterns to brighten the day;
And there are chestnuts ready for us to roast
Or cranberries from some distant coast.

Oh, it is good to store in the house and heart
The roadside stand's harvest wares ere they depart!

Earle J. Grant

Autumn
Stores

Like dreams wrapped in clouds, the things we remember
Drift slowly away and vanish from sight
Till some current of thought sweeps them clearly before us,
And we live them again in memory's light.

In the warm days of autumn, I think of the rides
To grandfather's mill at the end of the lane.
Farm horses went plodding, their brown heads nodding,
Patiently hauling the big bags of grain.
There was no hurry; as neighbors drove in,
Greetings and news were exchanged again.

What excitement there was when we found some wild honey!
Stored in the trunk of a hollow "bee tree"
Were great squares of honeycomb, rough and uneven,
Full of golden brown sweetness of rich quality.
Here was a treasure more precious than money,
A favorite treat for the whole family.

September and October brought their rich harvest.
Down in the cellar neath the woodshed floor,
Shelves were agleam with home-canned products;
Bins overflowed with their bounteous store.
The orchard's best apples would brighten the evenings
When we sat by the stove and heard winter's winds roar.

Like sunbeams on water, like rainbows in the blue,
Our remembrances shine a lifetime through.

Mary A. Selden

In the Warm Days of Autumn

Painting opposite:
NEARING HICKORY HILL
Ed Gifford

Overleaf
OTTAUQUECHEE RIVER, VERMONT
Cyr Color Photo

Nearing Hickory Hill
Ed Gifford

Out in the Country

in the Early Fall

Out in the country, in the early fall,
  When the trees change their summer array,
From a coat of bright green that they sported,
  To a number of colors, quite gay.

Here in the open, God's nature unveiled,
  Where a pauper can feel like a king;
And the air is so clean, it's enchanting,
  In the meadows where meadowlarks sing.

The clover and grass, a soft velvet mass,
  Hug the flowers that blush in the sun,
While the bees all day long, buzz their songs,
  Till they figure their day's work is done.

Across the green fields the crickets are heard,
  Singing out with their soft melody;
And wild geese wing their way to new places
  Far beyond what man's eyes can now see.

Then to bid adieu, neath a sky of blue,
To the natural things God has made,
Once again we take leave, ne'er forgetting,
All the beauty that fall has portrayed.

Anton J. Stoffle

Autumn Song

Sing a song of autumn,
 Apples sparkling bright,
Robins in the treetops
 Singing with delight.

Sing a song of chipmunks,
 And songs of meadowlarks,
Sing of squirrels a-chattering,
 Their tails all question marks.

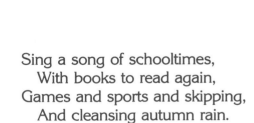

Sing a song of schooltimes,
 With books to read again,
Games and sports and skipping,
 And cleansing autumn rain.

Sing of homes and families,
 Of relatives and friends,
Sing of autumn's beauty
 And all the love God sends.

Lola Sneyd

Ernst Peterson

The Indian Stonecutter

As summer faded into autumn, many Indian tribes, especially the woodland tribes of middle and northeastern North America, prepared for their busiest time of year. Before the heavy snows of winter made hunting impossible, depleted summer larders had to be filled with dried and salted deer, bear, buffalo and antelope meat. When this time of year came, the persistent sound of rock hitting rock echoed through the quiet river valleys and towering mesas of America hundreds of years before the Puritans. This clatter meant the Indian stonecutter was making stone arrow and spear points for the upcoming autumn hunt.

The first step in making a stone tool or weapon, was to select the proper stones needed. For the small, light arrow points, the stonecutter looked for hard, but easily fracturable, stones, such as quartz, agate, flint or shale. After searching a nearby stream or protruding rock face for workable stones and pebbles, the craftsman returned to camp with a basketful of unlikely weapons. Yet, after a few days at the pounding rock, rough stones were honed into streamlined and useful implements.

To practice his craft, this primitive artisan's basic tools were a variety of hammerstones and a large pounding rock. He also used drills which he rubbed between his hands to wear a hole as needed. In addition, he had several pieces of sandstone for polishing, some flaking blades and a whetstone.

The stonecutter began with an angular piece of rock, perhaps quartz or agate, and pounded it with the heavy hammerstone until the rough oval core, or "spall" was attained. Then, with a smaller hammerstone, the stonecutter beat the edges of the rock to a thin edge. The two sides of the rock were then brought together in a point and the shape further defined. He then thinned or shaved the rock to give it a flattened appearance.

Now the stone had edge and evenness; all that remained was to beat or flake pieces from the sides of the stone until the desired shape was attained. Once accomplished, the stone was often notched at the "basal," or end, to create a stem which would nestle snuggly into the head of an arrow or spear. The size of the flakes and the position of the notches, or absence of them, were the trademarks of the various tribes.

In addition to hunting tools, the stonecutter made sturdy scrapers and axes to use later. When the hunt was over, meat had to be quartered, hides scraped and dried, and timber cut.

To make an axe or scraper, hard basalt and granite rocks were chosen. With these rocks, the stonecutter resorted to pounding, not flaking, giving the stone a pummelled look. Often, these larger weapons and tools were polished by rubbing them smooth with a piece of sandstone. Cutting, chopping and scraping edges were honed with the whetstone. Any necessary holes in the stone tool were laboriously made with the simple stone drills.

The stonecutter's work went on into the waning days of autumn. But as the first snows of winter beckoned the land to rest, and the hunters gradually relaxed their pursuit of quarry, the stonecutter, too, had time for more frivolous pursuits. Perhaps a request for a shell amulet or bone game was waiting, or the tribe's calumet needed repairing.

The time of relaxation would end, however; and the hearth fires would once more curl their pungent smoke far above the valleys and mesas. The time for the hunt would return, and the sound of the stonecutter's hammer would hail still another autumn.

The three stone objects in the center of the picture are examples of pummelled implements. These three, from left to right, are a celt, used in woodworking; a hide scraper, polished smooth with years of use; and an ancient axe head, used for felling trees. In the foreground are a number of flaked arrow points (note the difference in surface pattern between these and the pummelled tools above them). In the lower left-hand corner is a spear point. In the lower right-hand corner is a round, drilled stone which was probably used as a weight for fishing nets or as an ornament worn around the neck on a leather thong. These relics were unearthed near Lomira, Wisconsin. The bone game (below the celt), the shells and amulet (next to the drilled stone), bowls, rug, leather pouch and calumet pipe are all modern.

(Indian artifacts, courtesy Thunderbird Trading Post, Inc. Arrowhead collection, courtesy Kathy Weaver, Milwaukee, Wisconsin.)

THANKSGIVING

The Indian Maid has come and gone this year;
Her beaded moccasins of soft doeskin
Have crossed the fields, slipped through
   the wood, and paused
Beside the brook where purple asters grew;
And amethysts against her shining hair
Could never be as deep or royal. Swift
Her step, and strings of broken beads are strewn
Along the fence. In garlanded festive rows,
The scarlet bittersweet still clings to blaze
Her trail, and rounded sides of pumpkin gleam
Like balls of polished brass, half-buried where
The ground is silvered from the frost. A haze
Of woodsmoke hides the titian-colored hills,
And clouds of blanket-gray bed down the sun.
Those chevrons, black against the sky, are etched
By geese forsaking marshes, southward bound.
The Maid finds nests are empty where once grew
The fledglings. Fallow lies the land, asleep
Against the creeping cold. With one last look,
She steps beyond the fading day and soon
Is gone. But here the barns are full, and Man,
With stirrings in his heart of thankfulness,
Beholds the fruits of summer gathered in.
He stirs the fire, and sees the soaring sparks
As shooting stars that flare and flame. His roof
Is snug, his bed is warm, his children sing;
With deep content he smells the baking bread
And trims his lamp. Secure against the night
And rising wind, he knows within these walls
The winter holds no fear; for out beyond,
And all around, is God Who cares for him.

Alice Davis

Bright Gratitude

On rugged mountain passes
Reaching to the sky,
Grow timid quaking aspens
With tall green pines nearby.

The pines, in stately splendor
With guarding courage, send
Their strength and reassurance
To timid aspen friends.

But with coming on of autumn,
When summer days are old,
The aspens in bright gratitude
Pay them back in gold.

Eula Hardeman

October's Mountains

I stood on the top of a windblown hill,
  On a gold October day,
And fastened my gaze on the mountainside
  So many miles away.

The trees were bedecked in their gorgeous robes
  Of yellow and red and brown;
I felt as I stood there viewing them
  That I shared in their glad renown.

The sky was so blue, an azure blue,
  And the clouds were floating by;
I thought, only God makes the mountainsides
  And sighed a nostalgic sigh.

I stood on the top of a windblown hill
  And viewed the mountains afar;
October's mountains are ravishing,
  I love them for what they are!

Georgia B. Adams

Autumn in Your Hands

Hal Borland

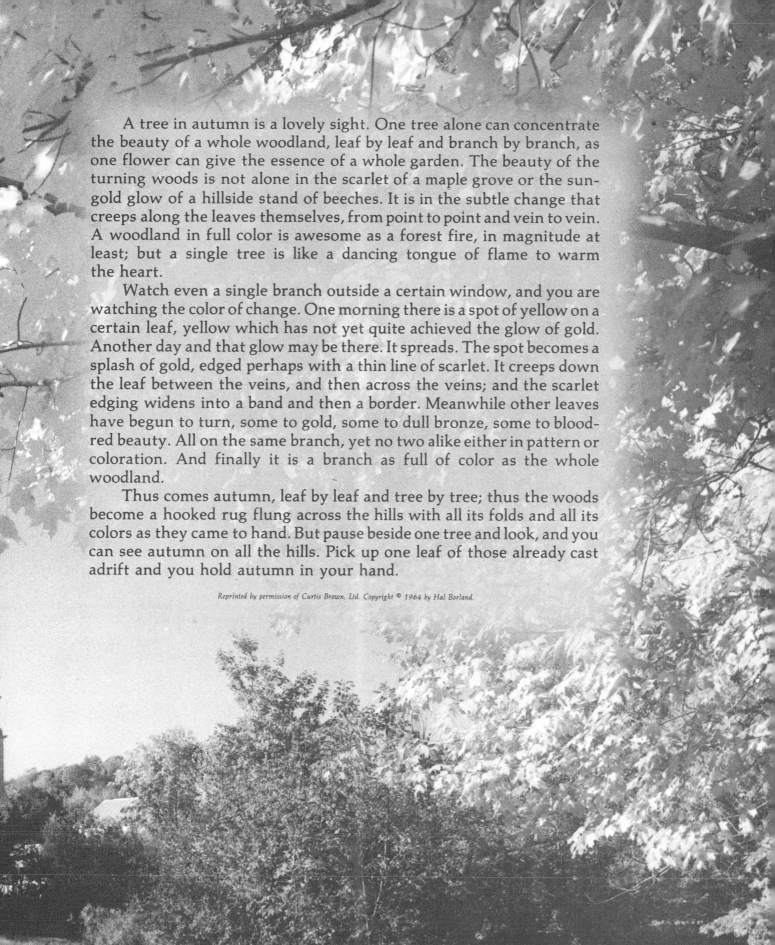

A tree in autumn is a lovely sight. One tree alone can concentrate the beauty of a whole woodland, leaf by leaf and branch by branch, as one flower can give the essence of a whole garden. The beauty of the turning woods is not alone in the scarlet of a maple grove or the sun-gold glow of a hillside stand of beeches. It is in the subtle change that creeps along the leaves themselves, from point to point and vein to vein. A woodland in full color is awesome as a forest fire, in magnitude at least; but a single tree is like a dancing tongue of flame to warm the heart.

Watch even a single branch outside a certain window, and you are watching the color of change. One morning there is a spot of yellow on a certain leaf, yellow which has not yet quite achieved the glow of gold. Another day and that glow may be there. It spreads. The spot becomes a splash of gold, edged perhaps with a thin line of scarlet. It creeps down the leaf between the veins, and then across the veins; and the scarlet edging widens into a band and then a border. Meanwhile other leaves have begun to turn, some to gold, some to dull bronze, some to blood-red beauty. All on the same branch, yet no two alike either in pattern or coloration. And finally it is a branch as full of color as the whole woodland.

Thus comes autumn, leaf by leaf and tree by tree; thus the woods become a hooked rug flung across the hills with all its folds and all its colors as they came to hand. But pause beside one tree and look, and you can see autumn on all the hills. Pick up one leaf of those already cast adrift and you hold autumn in your hand.

Autumn is a basket
With golden ripened grain,
Red and yellow apples
Bejeweled with drops of rain.
Purple clustered grapes
Scent the crisp new morn,
Bouquets of late flowers
Its edges to adorn.
Autumn is a basket
Where Jack Frost nimbly weaves
The crimson of the sumac
With brown and golden leaves.
A moon for a handle
Spiked with twinkling stars,
Lined with Indian summer days,
The beauty of which is ours!

Hazel Elizabeth Park

The reds and golds of autumn
  still linger on the hill,
As we gather nature's bounties,
  our depleted stores to fill.

Some wild geese still are sailing,
  alert, the wild birds flush,
The hunter's at his trailing,
  the artist seeks his brush.
At night the stars seem closer,
  the trees still hold their fire
Till winter winds play havoc
  with leaves we now admire.

When we pause from daily strivings
  and give thought to our gifts,
Our homes, our work, our families,
  quite soon our vision lifts
To God, before whose harvest
  all man-made things decrease.
Our humble hearts are grateful
  that still His gifts increase.

We take stock of our blessings,
  viewing one more harvest's hoard,
And we bow in thankful reverence
  at the table of the Lord.

Alice Leedy Mason

The Leaf Painter

David Hoxworth

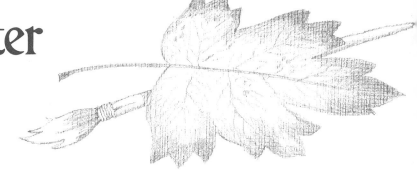

The late afternoon sun was just beginning to fall behind the distant hills. The Indian youths sat around the fire with the old wise one of the tribe, Dreamspinner.

The braves were all out hunting to be sure of a food supply for the winter ahead. The Indian women were gathering berries, roots, and wood to help keep them through the coming winter months.

On the hillsides, the sun's rays glistened from the mixture of the colored trees. The effect was almost like a continuous rainbow, with the many patches of orange, yellow, brown, and in the higher regions, the deep green of the pine and spruce trees. The village seemed surrounded by the beauty and the greatness of nature.

The fire crackled as the youths sat around playing their games and listening to the tribe's teller of tales, Dreamspinner. The joking and the gentle stillness was broken when the young brave, Swift Fox, turned to the ancient one and asked, "Dreamspinner, why are all the trees so different? Some of the trees are yellow, others brown, and others almost red—and yet the pine, spruce, and cedar trees are green, and stay green all winter."

Dreamspinner raised his head, the smoke slowly curling from his pipe. His eyes seemed distant, as if he were somewhere else.

When Dreamspinner began his tale, his voice was low, but clear. "In the beginning was the Great Spirit, and the Great Spirit created everything. However, the Great Spirit did have many lesser spirits which helped him in many of his jobs. One of these spirits was called the Growth Spirit. This spirit was the spirit of the

time that you now know of as spring. Another helper was called the Heat Spirit, or as it is now called, summer. The spirit that is responsible for that which you ask me, and of which I will tell you shortly, is the spirit called the Leaf Painter. And, of course, the final spirit was that of the Cold Maker."

Dreamspinner was quiet for a while, then he took another puff from his pipe. His voice carried over the silence. "But you asked me why the leaves of some trees are so many different colors, yet certain trees remain green all year round. Well, in the beginning, after Growth Spirit and Heat Spirit had finished their work, it came time for the Leaf Painter to begin his. The Leaf Painter was a most famous artist, and the major tasks of Leaf Painter were to dry the foods produced by Growth and Heat Spirit, and to make the countryside beautiful.

"Leaf Painter's paints were made from things of the earth. He had to mix soils, berries, and juices from roots of plants. The Leaf Painter mixed the different brown dirts to make a bright brown. He found some berries and flowers which he squeezed to get a brilliant yellow. He gathered some red clay and mixed it, making an orange red color. Finally, he took some different berries and made purple."

Dreamspinner seemed lost in another world as he continued: "Now you must remember that Leaf Painter was a mighty spirit and a great artist. He began work immediately. With a few sweeps of his hands he was able to paint a complete oak tree, turning its leaves to hues of golden brown. However, there were many oak trees, and this work took several days. Leaf Painter next moved to the beautiful aspen and birch trees. After much thought he decided that these should be a beautiful yellow, which would blend well with the golden browns he had already created. He took his yellow paints and worked several more days painting all the birch and aspen. As I have said, Leaf Painter was a great artist, and the results were striking. They came out a sparkling yellow, and he was proud of his work. He next thought of the maple and the sumac, He decided to make them a bright orange red. Taking his paints, he worked several more days painting these trees.

"Now all that was left was for Leaf Painter to move farther up into the hills, where the pine, spruce, and cedar grew most abundantly. Leaf Painter had decided that these should be the color of purple. However, since he had worked several days, he chose to rest before climbing the steep hills.

"The next morning Leaf Painter went far up the hillside until he came to the mighty pine. He made one swipe at the pine tree with his hand. But the long, thin needles jammed into his fingers, causing them to bleed. He tried from a different direction, but no matter how he approached the tree, or how he tried, the needles stuck in his fingers, hurting him so badly he was unable to continue.

"The next morning his hands felt some- what better

and he decided to try the spruce and the cedar. However, exactly the same thing happened. Leaf Painter's hands were sore and bleeding. And he was deeply puzzled as to how to paint these trees. So, since he had been working very hard those past several weeks, he decided to return to his tepee for a few days to think, to rest, and to let his hands heal.

"During the night a gentle rain fell. In the morning, when Leaf Painter awoke, he went out to get some water in which to soak his sore hands. As he glanced upon the hillside, he saw the mixture of beautiful brown oak, yellow aspen and birch, the orange red sumac and maple, but also in the distance he saw the glistening of the water droplets from the dark green pine, spruce, and cedar. Leaf Painter stood back. He felt that this was right and beautiful and decided to leave them as they were."

The crackling fire was all that broke the stillness as Dreamspinner dropped his head. He took a long puff from his pipe, then raised his head and once more viewed the beauty of the surrounding hills.

The Indian youths quietly rose to go to their own tepees, to dream their own dreams of being great hunters, mighty warriors, or even famous artists, like Leaf Painter.

Landing of the Pilgrim Fathers

The breaking waves dashed high
On the stern and rock-bound coast;
And the woods against the stormy sky,
Their giant branches tossed.

And the heavy night hung dark
The hills and waters o'er,
When a band of exiles moored their bark
On the wild New England shore.

Not as the conqueror comes,
They, the true-hearted came.
Not with the roll of the stirring drums,
And the trumpet that sings of fame;

Not as the flying come,
In silence and in fear;
They shook the depths of the desert gloom
With their hymns of lofty cheer.

Amid the storms they sang,
And the stars heard, and the sea;
And the sounding aisles of the dim woods rang
To the anthem of the free.

The ocean eagle soared
From his nest by the white wave's foam;
And the rocking pines of the forest roared;
This was their welcome home.

There were men with hoary hair
Amid that pilgrim band:
Why had they come to wither there,
Away from their childhood's land?

There was woman's fearless eye,
Lit by her deep love's truth;
There was manhood's brow, serenely high,
And the fiery heart of youth.

What sought they thus afar?
Bright jewels of the mine?
The wealth of seas, the spoils of war?
They sought a faith's pure shrine!

Ay, call it holy ground,
The spot where first they trod;
They left unstained what there they found:
Freedom to worship God.

Felicia D. Hemans

Painting opposite
LANDING OF THE PILGRIMS

ANNE BRADSTREET: New World Poet

Seven years after the *Mayflower* landed at Plymouth Rock, another ship docked a few miles to the south at Salem, Massachusetts. This vessel, the *Arabella,* was the flagship of John Winthrop's fleet. When the passengers disembarked, America's first poet, Anne Dudley Bradstreet had arrived.

Anne Bradstreet was just seventeen when she came to the New World with her parents, Thomas and Sarah Dudley, and her husband of two years, Simon Bradstreet. She had led the genteel and ordered life of the daughter of a wealthy steward. In England, Dudley had managed the vast estates of the Earl of Lincoln, and the Dudley family lived in the Earl's Tattersall Castle. Here, the young Anne Dudley studied under the best tutors available and had access to the Earl's vast library. Nothing, however, could have prepared her for conditions in Massachusetts that summer of 1627.

Thomas Dudley recorded the state of the settlement upon their arrival: "Our four ships which set out in April arrived here in June and July, where we found the Colony in a sad and unexpected condition, above eighty of them being dead the winter before; and many of those alive weak and sick; all the corn and bread amongst them all hardly sufficient to feed them a fortnight. . . . Salem, where we landed pleased us not."

It is no wonder that Anne Bradstreet later wrote of that arrival: "I . . . came into this Country, where I found a new world and new manners, at which my heart rose. But after I was convinced it was the way of God, I submitted to it and joined to the church at Boston." This ability to submit to what she felt to be God's will characterized her life and poetry.

During the next eight years, the Bradstreets moved into four houses until they were permanently settled at Andover, a city north of Boston. Mrs. Bradstreet's life in the New World was as the daughter and wife of two of the most influential men in the Colony. Her father became the second governor of Massachusetts and her husband was a permanent member of the Court of Assistants.

Bradstreet was often away from home helping arbitrate disputes among the colonists. Mrs. Bradstreet was left alone on the edge of the wilderness to tend their eight children, accomplish various household duties, and fend off both disease and Indians. There is nothing in her poetry to indicate she feared either.

She wrote poetry, not in idleness, but as a serious pursuit. Her first collection of poetry, *The Tenth Muse, Lately Sprung Up In America,* was published in London in 1650 by her brother-in-law. This early poetry is pedantic, impersonal and generally uninteresting. She said of this publication, no doubt anticipating criticism from Puritans less appreciative of her art than her family: "Theyl say my hand a needle better fits." She persisted, however, in revising the early works and writing new poems.

The later works, published after her death, are generally regarded as her best. Writing of her family, home and faith, a view of everyday life in an early Puritan colony emerges as in no other contemporary work. She did all this in an environment from which any literary output would be astounding, from a woman, unthinkable.

Perhaps part of the reason for her success lies in the person and attitude of Simon Bradstreet. Much of her poetry is about him, to him, and probably because of him. His portrait shows, not the harsh Puritan of a Hawthorne novel, but a gentle face, curling mustache and slightly rotund figure. He evoked this loving tribute from his wife:

If ever two were one, then surely we.
If ever man were loved by wife, then thee;
If ever wife was happy in a man,
Compare with me, ye women, if you can.

Anne Bradstreet is incomparable. During her lifetime she minded her children, tended her home and husband, and honored her God. There is no extant portrait of her; but because of her, a panorama emerges of early New England and those Puritans who influenced this country as no other group ever could. Her legacy chronicles the characteristic that insured the survival of these strangers in a strange land: love of both man and God. On this foundation, Anne Bradstreet laid the literary cornerstone of a nation.

New York Public Library

IN REFERENCE TO HER CHILDREN,
23 June, 1659

I had eight birds hatched in one nest,
Four cocks there were, and hens the rest.
I nursed them up with pain and care,
Nor cost, nor labour did I spare,
Till at the last they felt their wing,
Mounted the trees, and learned to sing;

* * *

Meanwhile my days in tunes I'll spend,
Till my weak lays with me shall end.
In shady woods I'll sit and sing,
And things that past to mind I'll bring.

* * *

And from the top bough take my flight
Into a country beyond sight,
Where old ones instantly grow young,
And there with seraphims set song;
No seasons cold, nor storms they see;
But spring lasts to eternity.

* * *

Farewell, my birds, farewell adieu,
I happy am, if well with you.

A. B.

I'm thankful, Lord, for those great men
Who braved the seas to win this land;
Their sacrifices fill our history's pages.
Unfortunately, they couldn't know
That their heroic lives bestowed
Freedom to this nation through the ages.

For such a time, they each one served
Nor from their dauntless purpose swerved
From contribution to the cause of liberty.
Those Pilgrim Fathers never dreamt
What to the world their struggles meant
Or, that they fulfilled their country's destiny.

I Give Thanks

My earnest prayer that I may too,
By life I live, the things I do,
Be mindful of mankind's eternal aim.
Some small thing that men may see
Within this world because of me
A little better than before I came.
If I can smooth the path for those
Who travel after, in the throes

Of a world in change, a future none can see.
If, hopefully, while I am here
Within my small self-centered sphere,
I can do this. Lord, I give thanks to Thee!

Eugene D. Tilley

The charming Pilgrim dolls featured opposite are creations of Betty Brown of Mequon, Wisconsin.

Paths that Lead Toward Home

I guess perhaps it's natural
   To want to travel far
And to visit in strange places
   Where new adventures are.
I guess some paths lead to pleasure
   In north, south, east and west;
But the paths that lead toward home
   Most truly are the best.

Perhaps distance lends enchantment,
   Perhaps it may be true,
That something bright and wonderful
   Awaits afar for you.
Yet whatever paths you travel,
   There is one thing I know;
You seek paths that lead toward home
   No matter where you go.

Virginia Katherine Oliver

Home for Thanksgiving

Home is where I long to be
On this Thanksgiving Day;
Home . . . with all the heart of me,
So many miles away.

The family will be gathered there;
I can see their dear sweet faces
Around the table bowed in prayer . . .
The old familiar places.

The crackling hearth is glowing,
Flames reflected on the floor;
I can hear the young folks singing
As I sang in years before.

There's a road that leads me homeward,
In my heart there is a prayer
That the miles go swift behind me
And I'll spend Thanksgiving there.

Mildred L. Jarrell

We Gather Together

Translated from the Dutch by THEODORE BAKER   Traditional tune arranged by EDWARD KREMSER

1. We gath - er to - geth - er to ask the Lord's bless - ing;
2. Be - side us to guide us, our God with us join - ing,
3. We all do ex - tol Thee, Thou Lead - er tri - um - phant,

He chas - tens and has - tens His will to make known;
Or - dain - ing, main - tain - ing His king - dom di - vine;
And pray that Thou still our De - fend - er wilt be.

The wick - ed op - press - ing now cease from dis - tress - ing;
So from the be - gin - ning the fight we were win - ning;
Let Thy con - gre - ga - tion es - cape trib - u - la - tion;

Sing prais - es to His Name, He for - gets not His own.
Thou, Lord, wast at our side, all glo - ry be Thine.
Thy Name be ev - er praised! O Lord, Make us free! A - men.

The colonists may have been many things, but, it would appear, they were not very romantic. While basking in the soft glow of candlelight, prized so highly today, they complained bitterly about the taper's congenital inefficiencies: foul smell, "fuliginous smoak," and expense. They understood with Ben Franklin that the frugal, sensible person went "early to bed and early to rise" principally to conserve his candles and his eyes, not only for the moral uplift.

Perhaps to offset the frustrations of the candle, the holder was a carefully conceived instrument that made the most of its candlepower. Reading fixtures concentrated two or three candles close together. Wall sconces, intended for dispersing light over a wider area, were backed up with a variety of reflecting materials.

Because of their long history and the variety of materials used, candleholders offer a challenging and reasonably priced specialty for the new collector. Most of the examples shown on these pages are unique works and virtually unpriceable, but the persistent seeker can discover period pieces from a few dollars up. Choice finds occur in the $100 to $150 range, especially at auctions where prices tend to be lower. Before starting to buy seriously, however, the beginning collector should first develop some knowledge of the subject. Joseph T. Butler's *Candleholders in America* (published by Crown, 1967) would be a fine start. At the same time a good eye for spotting fakes, which means learning about the hand-manufacturing techniques of earlier days, would be helpful. Both are part of the fun of becoming a collector.

A Gallery of American
CANDLESTICKS

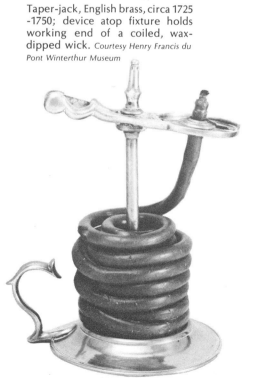

Taper-jack, English brass, circa 1725 -1750; device atop fixture holds working end of a coiled, wax-dipped wick. *Courtesy Henry Francis du Pont Winterthur Museum*

Round brass chamber stick with beaded edges and push slide with large rectangular openings to admit snuffers. Scrolled handle has maker's mark on thumbpiece; square opening is to hang extinquisher. Circa 1760. *Old Sturbridge Village Photo*

Clear pressed-glass candlestick with square base, dolphin shaft and patterned cup, circa 1830-1845. *Old Sturbridge Village Photo*

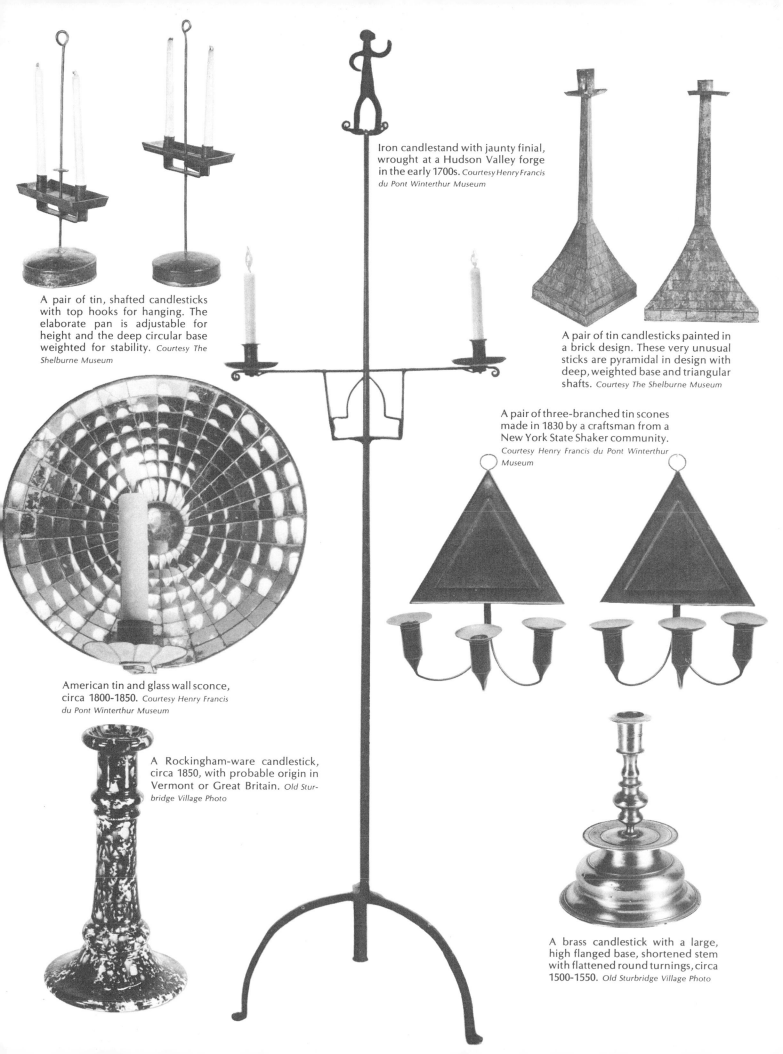

A pair of tin, shafted candlesticks with top hooks for hanging. The elaborate pan is adjustable for height and the deep circular base weighted for stability. *Courtesy The Shelburne Museum*

Iron candlestand with jaunty finial, wrought at a Hudson Valley forge in the early 1700s. *Courtesy Henry Francis du Pont Winterthur Museum*

A pair of tin candlesticks painted in a brick design. These very unusual sticks are pyramidal in design with deep, weighted base and triangular shafts. *Courtesy The Shelburne Museum*

A pair of three-branched tin sconces made in 1830 by a craftsman from a New York State Shaker community. *Courtesy Henry Francis du Pont Winterthur Museum*

American tin and glass wall sconce, circa 1800-1850. *Courtesy Henry Francis du Pont Winterthur Museum*

A Rockingham-ware candlestick, circa 1850, with probable origin in Vermont or Great Britain. *Old Sturbridge Village Photo*

A brass candlestick with a large, high flanged base, shortened stem with flattened round turnings, circa 1500-1550. *Old Sturbridge Village Photo*

Thanksgiving Time

I'm thankful for so many things.
   It's hard to pick out just a few
And tell, in little simple words,
   How very much they mean to you.

First there is sunlight rich and warm
   Shining upon the house and lot;
The good laws of our native land,
   For which our fathers lived and fought.

For neighbors just beyond the fence,
   Whose lives are closely linked with ours,
With whom we share so many things:
   Driveways and lights and growing flowers.

For crops of grain, for fruit and meat,
   The fragrance of the earth, the trees,
Churches, schools and country lanes,
   I am so thankful for all these.

For children in a hundred schools,
   For timid old folks bent and worn,
Young mothers, brave as knights of old,
   Waiting for babies to be born.

For old church bells that softly chime,
A turkey at Thanksgiving time.

Edna Jaques

Memories of Yesterday

The falling leaves of red and gold,
  Swept by the autumn breeze,
Drift quietly across the fields
  Where they rest in perfect ease.
As the sunset's hues are spreading
  Deep colors there on high,
Tall trees are silhouetted
  Against the western sky.

The covered bridge across the stream,
  Once so busy in its day,
Is covered now with cool green moss
  And falling to decay.
The creaking mill which once had turned,
  Throwing far the sparkling spray,
Is silent now; and its beauty,
  A memory of yesterday.

Margaret Louise Mints

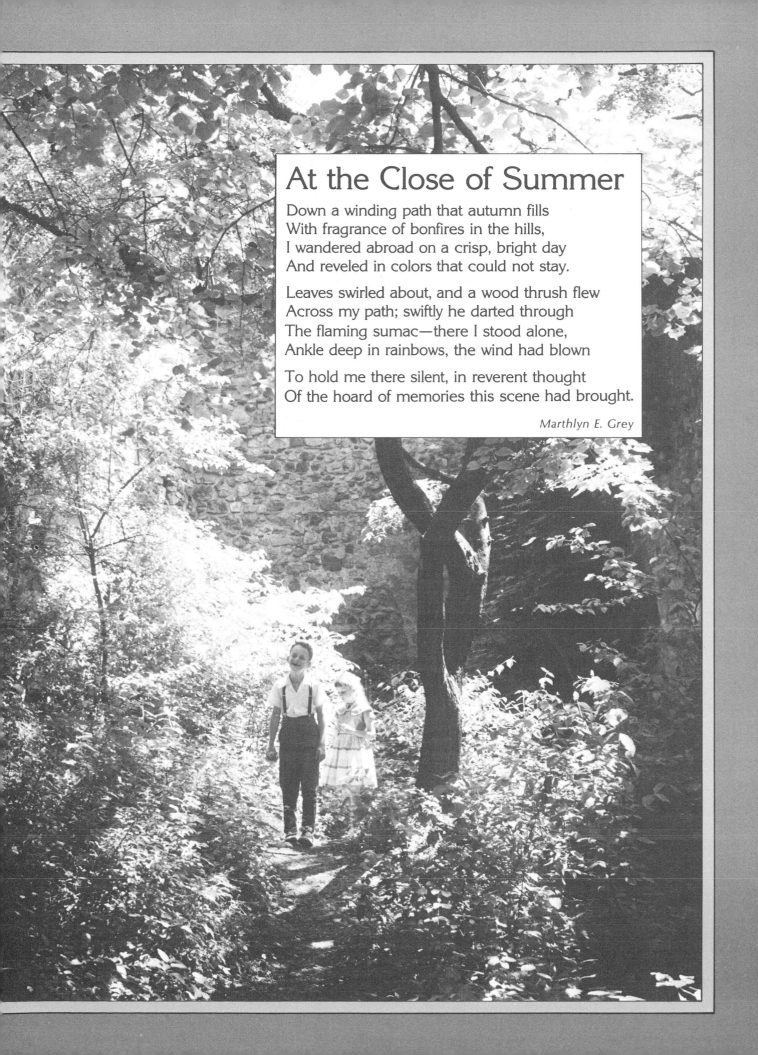

At the Close of Summer

Down a winding path that autumn fills
With fragrance of bonfires in the hills,
I wandered abroad on a crisp, bright day
And reveled in colors that could not stay.

Leaves swirled about, and a wood thrush flew
Across my path; swiftly he darted through
The flaming sumac—there I stood alone,
Ankle deep in rainbows, the wind had blown

To hold me there silent, in reverent thought
Of the hoard of memories this scene had brought.

Marthlyn E. Grey

Treasures

My home is full of treasures
  That mean so much to me.
They wouldn't be considered
  As rare antiquity—

Bits of hand embroidery,
  Made with utmost care,
Pictures, gifts and well-worn books,
  A baby's rocking chair.

My heart is full of memories
  Tenderly stored away,
But in secret I can take them out
  And enjoy them day by day.

The store is richer, rarer,
  With each swiftly passing year,
For every added treasure
  Makes them all more dear.

My life is full of friendships,
  Each treasured one unique,
For when I need uplifting,
  A certain friend I seek.

And when I need some comforting,
  From one who understands,
There's always strength and courage
  In the press of that one's hands.

My days are full of duties,
  Some are dreary, others gay,
I often wish to change the plan
  Were there any other way,

But when I just remember
  There's something for each need,
Although I'm poor in worldly goods,
  I know I'm rich, indeed.

Margaretta Brown

Photo opposite: Multicolored "Granny" afghan (size 45" x 60"). To order kit containing yarn and instructions, mail $13.95 to Ideals Publishing Corp., 11315 Watertown Plank Road, Milwaukee, Wis. 53226.

Another Season

Gray embers smoke the last of autumn's blaze;
Browned, final leaves cling, trembling, to the boughs
Laid bare, in silhouette against the sky
Of chill November's pewter-clouded days.
White-breasted sea gulls reel and dip and soar,
Sleek, graceful, clean and sweeping in their flight;
They turn their wings against the high-blown winds,
And cast their lonely shadows on the shore.
The first light snowflakes frost the cooling earth;
Gray evening shadows call an early dusk.
We watch another season burning low,
And at the twilight, turn to home and hearth.

Rena Przychocki

November Stillness

November is a quiet month
  That holds its breath, it seems,
While Mother Earth prepares the land
  For winter's lengthy dreams.

No longer do the doors of home
  Admit the charms of spring . . .
No longer do we hear the songs
  Of birds who gaily sing.

The silence of the wintertime
  Descends on one and all
The silent stars in quiet sky . . .
  The muted snows that fall.

And in the stillness of it all
  As stars look down and nod
I hear the Psalmist say "Be still
  And know that I am God."

Carice Williams

In a November Field

God, listening now above all autumn fields
That, vastly silent, pray,
Hear, in this field, the prayer of thankfulness
My little words would say.
I have come out from walled-in-house and
　　church
To feel November's sun . . .
To place my feet upon this quiet ground
Whose harvesting is done.
You who look kindly on these dull, stacked
　　husks
And see in them frail seeds,
Fresh, trembling shoots; then sturdy corn that
　　gave
Its strength to meet man's needs—
See in my weariness some work well done;
The thought, the eager toil,
And altruism grown from self as plants
Grew green from the drab soil.

You who know well this field but rests awhile
That it may once more be
Prepared to give again, teach me to rest
Thus, God, unselfishly.
You who, at harvest's end, when autumn's
　　sheen
Is tarnished and the white
Of winter has not cleansed the earth, still keep
Round pumpkins, yellow-bright
Among dry sheaves, wise God, keep laughter's
　　gold
In my tired heart today . . .
That, with the joyful wisdom of this field,
I, too, may stand and pray.

Violet Alleyn Storey

Photo opposite
John Vondell

Peeping out from in between
Autumn trees that still are green,
Are leaves of tangerine and gold;
Such beauty never does grow old!
Against a sky of azure blue
Are leaves of many other hue:
Lemon, honey, orange and lime,
Who doesn't love the autumn time?

Agnes Finch Whitacre

ACKNOWLEDGMENTS

COUNTRY CELLAR by Mary Louise Cheatham. Previously published in THE LYRIC, Fall 1963. LITTLE SPUNK OF HALLOWEEN HOLLOW by Arlene Cook. Previously published in ANIMAL CAVALCADE. Used with permission of the author. A WILD APPLE by Reid Crowell. Used by permission.

Additional photo credits: Inside front cover, Waits River, Vermont, Fred Sieb. Inside back cover, Richard W. Brown

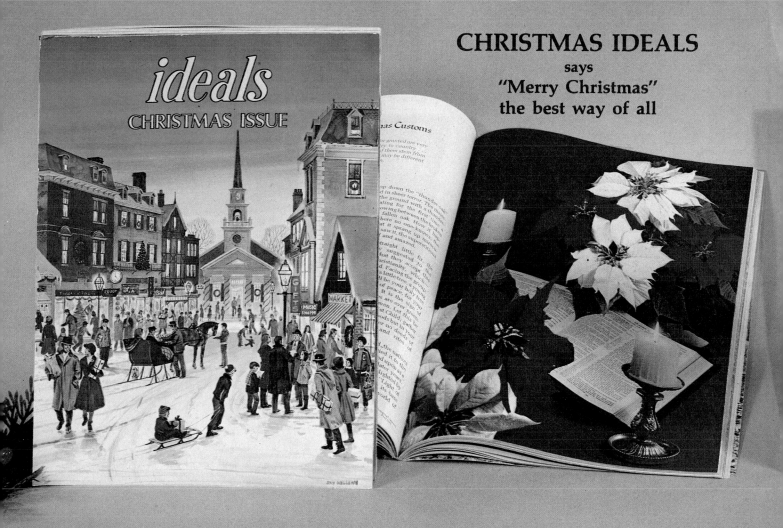

CHRISTMAS IDEALS
says
"Merry Christmas"
the best way of all

CHRISTMAS IDEALS
is
The glitter of the tinsel . . .
The sparkle of the snow—
The Blessings of the season
And the hearthside's warmest glow

You'll enjoy every wonderful aspect of the most welcome season of the year in the beautiful pages of CHRISTMAS IDEALS. Nothing will put you and your loved ones in the mood for Christmas faster—and keep you in this happy frame of mind longer—than the arrival of CHRISTMAS IDEALS. Through its unequaled presentation of seasonal poetry, prose, artwork and photography, readers will discover and cherish the true joys of Christmases past and present. You will want to share this loving gift of precious and lasting thoughts of the Christmas season with family and friends alike.

In the new 1977 CHRISTMAS IDEALS you will revere the ageless miracle of the Nativity through the breathtaking paintings by the Old Masters. You'll enjoy many a delightful article, such as "America's Sled and Sleigh Days," artistically accented with a full color Currier & Ives reproduction. And something for the children, too, a fascinating feature on how various small animals spend their winters.

Readers will go on to enjoy an illustrated look at old-time Christmas cards . . . a factual and fanciful piece on the delicate beauty of snowflakes . . . and young and old alike will learn a most precious answer to the question, "Is There A Santa Claus?" And all this wealth of Christmas material is yours in a publication without advertising. Your friends and family will love CHRISTMAS IDEALS 1977 as much as you do. Use the convenient order blank enclosed and make sure you get several copies of a great Christmas remembrance. Only $2.50. Softcover—Actual size 8½ x 11".
Special Hardcover Library Edition Only $5.00

FRIENDSHIP—Thoughtful messages in poetry and prose combine with the full color beauty of charming photos in a moving and memorable tribute to friendship as God had meant it to be—a thing of giving . . . caring . . . sharing. Hardcover—80 Pages—Only $3.95

IN THE BEGINNING—A photographic interpretation of the seven days of creation. Each evolving day and the related creations are movingly reflected upon by classic authors and poets, accented with passages from the Bible. A book devoted to a greater understanding of God's work. Hardcover—64 pages—Only $3.95

BECAUSE YOU ARE MY FRIEND—The hearwarming sincerity that embodies the word friendship is colorfully and beautifully expressed as artwork and photos combine with words of friendship in a modern-day presentation. Hardcover—80 Pages—Only $5.00

LET'S BE FRIENDS—A daily guide to getting along with people providing a more meaningful understanding of personal situations encountered along life's way, as presented by Rev. Nathanael Olson. A gift book of light, pleasurable reading, yet inspiringly sincere. Hardcover—64 Pages—Only $3.50

A KEEPSAKE—Here's a beautiful book of prose and poetry that radiates the wondrous works of the master inspirational poets—covering a wide variety of subjects of the heart and soul. A special gift for someone special. Hardcover—80 Pages—Only $3.75

LOVE IS . . . OH, SO MANY THINGS—Colorful and creative photography expresses love's timeless moments in a contemporary way. It captures the magic moods of people in love and the love found in the wonders of nature around us. Hardcover—80 Pages—Only $5.00

BEST LOVED POEMS FROM IDEALS—All which is beautiful to the eye, comforting to the spirit and tender to the heart is found among the inspiring pages of this outstanding collection of poems. Beautifully accented throughout with 20 color photos. Hardcover—80 Pages—Only $3.95

A MOTHER IS LOVE—All the love, devotion and compassion you feel and those thoughts you find difficult to express can be found among the lovely pages of this beautiful keepsake collection of prose, poetry and photos for and about Mothers. Hardcover—64 Pages—Only $3.75

MOMENTS TO TREASURE—A perfect reflection of those moments in life that often are passed by unnoticed and yet are the substance of our days, providing warmth, happiness and inspiration. Warmly highlighted with charming artwork and color photos. Hardcover—80 Pages—Only $3.50

COUNT ONLY THE SUNNY HOURS—A gift book reflecting a general theme of the timeless moments of love, friendship, the cycle of life and the everlasting beauties of nature which they embrace is inspiringly presented in precious word and photography. Hardcover—80 Pages—Only $3.75

OUND BOOKS
d Year Round Reading Pleasure

SCRAPBOOK FAVORITES—Ideals' all-time favorite expressions of the seasons, holidays and the magnificent scenery of our country in poetry, prose and colorful pictures. It's a beautiful gift for any occasion. Hardcover—80 Pages—Only $2.95

A BOOK OF MEMORIES—A nostalgic presentation of colorful photos and artwork enriched with charming poetry in appreciation of the simpler things in life in years gone by. A gift book for quiet reflection and comforting memories. Hardcover—80 Pages—Only $2.95

THE PASSING SCENE—A nostalgic glimpse into the past presenting pictures of family life, colorful advertisements, autos . . . all the things that were a part of American life during the period from the 1900's to the 30's. Hardcover—80 Pages—Only $3.50

THE PEACEABLE KINGDOM—Poetry and prose of famous naturalists blend with colorful nature photos of animals from around the globe to portray the peace and unity among the world's unique creatures. A gift book of inspiration and beauty. Hardcover—64 Pages—Only $3.75

WOODLAND PORTRAITS—Thirty art reproductions of Harry Moeller's famous paintings of wildlife, each suitable for framing, are beautifully combined with the inspirationally informative writings of the well-known wildlife author, Sam Campbell. Hardcover—80 Pages—Only $3.95

WAYSIDE FLOWERS—Sparkling color photos and enriching verse harmoniously present the viewing of nature and the truth and wisdom that we share in life, to give added meaning to the past and hope for the future. Hardcover—64 Pages—Only $3.75

THE AMERICAN ALBUM—Read the motivating messages, in both poetry and prose, of such noted Americans as: Walt Whitman, Mark Twain, Harriet Beecher Stowe, F.D.R. and many others. An excellent combination of information and inspiration. Hardcover—80 Pages—Only $3.95

STORIES CHILDREN LOVE—Filled with exceptionally beautiful full color photographs and illustrations, here's a delightful collection of entertaining stories and poems that will capture the heart and imagination of every young reader. Hardcover—80 Pages—Only $3.50

STORYBOOK FAVORITES—Stories that have fascinated children for many years, Cinderella, Hansel and Gretel, The Pied Piper of Hamelin are just a few children will enjoy and delight in reading and rereading. For bedtime, playtime, anytime. Hardcover—80 Pages—Only $3.00

Larger Books 8½" x 11"
Smaller Books 7" x 9⅞"

Christmas Begins And Never Ends With A Subscription To IDEALS

Here is the story of the real America, the good-news stories of down-to-earth Americans and the solid ideas and ideals they live by. Each issue of IDEALS includes a beautiful collection of full color photos—nature, people, homes, interiors, antiques—art reproductions that almost jump off the page, poetry, unusual stories and articles, and stories in pictures of the almost forgotten crafts of yesterday.

And every sparkling page of an IDEALS is absolutely free from distracting advertisements!

IDEALS is much more than a magazine . . . it's a delightful visit with the people who have made our country great—a renewed statement of faith in the customs, beliefs and purposes of yesterday. With each issue of IDEALS, keyed to the season, you discover anew the wonderful world of our fathers, of their regard for one another, of the honesty and love and steadfast belief in the good life.

There's color, pages and pages of glorious color scenes from all over America and around the world—the kind of photos you will want to frame and keep forever for sheer pleasure. But IDEALS is much more than a beautiful magazine. It's filled with stories and verse about the things and people and customs that have made our country great. It tells about the purposes and beliefs and daily lives of good people everywhere.

Future Issues To Be Enjoyed And Shared In The Months Ahead For Subscribers To Ideals

Jan.-Feb. 1978—FIRESIDE
IDEALS—contains themes of home, friendship, country, winter's beauty. You'll enjoy a writing by Carl Sandburg on Abe Lincoln; a special feature on chess collections along with many more fine articles for year round reading enjoyment.

March-Apr. 1978—EASTER
IDEALS embraces the religious significance of the season and the awakening of nature in the springtime. You'll enjoy the story background of Charles Wesley's hymn, "Christ The Lord Is Risen Today," and thrill to the beauty of springtime in the Rockies in "Wildflowers."

Every bimonthly issue of IDEALS brings more surprises and stories you'll want to save. That's why thousands of long time subscribers still have every issue they ever received. No one throws away IDEALS. It's too good a friend and companion to ever wear out its welcome.

And we are so sure you'll feel this way about IDEALS that we proudly extend to every new subscriber our personal

MONEY BACK GUARANTEE

If, after receiving the first copy on your subscription, you find IDEALS is not as beautiful and inspiring as you expected, just return your copy to us in its original wrapper marked "return to sender." We will cancel your subscription and the invoice due.

So strengthen your faith in country, home and the American way of life through the beautiful pages of IDEALS—enter your subscription today! You needn't send any money now unless you prefer. Simply mark the proper area on the order blank and we'll bill you later.

IDEALS SUBSCRIPTION PLANS

ONE YEAR........6 issues as published $10.00
   (A saving of $5.00 under the single copy rate.)

TWO YEAR........12 issues as published....................$17.00
   (A saving of $13.00 under the single copy rate.)

THREE YEAR........18 issues as published.................$24.00
   (A saving of $21.00 under the single copy rate.)

4 VOLUME........4 issues as published ....$ 7.50
   (A saving of $2.50 under the single copy rate.)

PAY AS YOU READ PLAN
$2.00 per copy

Use the Pay-As-You-Read Plan: 1. Send no money now. 2. Expect the current issue, or any title you designate, by return mail, with an invoice and return envelope. 3. Remit $2.00 by return mail. 4. The next issue will be sent automatically; you needn't reorder each time. If you want to cancel your pay-as-you-read subscription, notify us at least three weeks before publication date.

IDEALS
1978 PUBLICATION SCHEDULE

Fireside Ideals.. Jan.
Easter Ideals.. Mar.
Neighborly Ideals .... May
Countryside Ideals.. July
Thanksgiving Ideals .... Sept.
Christmas Ideals .... Nov.

"Bound To Be Beautiful"
IDEALS BINDER

As rich looking as the six issues it holds with metal rods that eliminate punching. Stiff royal blue leather-cloth cover, embossed in gold. Yours for only $4.00. Hardcover 8½ x 11 inches.